How to Write a Book

And Make At Least Six Hundred Dollars

By Rocco Tenaglia III

Cover by Brad Roelandt

Images by Brad Roelandt, Rocco Tenaglia III, and Tony Tenaglia

Special thanks to Jacqui Swartz, Jeremy Medina, and Zack Newkirk

Printed in the United States of America

First Printing, 2019

Published by Bazizio Press
1041 N Formosa Ave.
West Hollywood, CA

For Jacqui, my sick wife

CONTENTS

INTRODUCTION

There are two types of Writer.

There is the Writer who lives to put words on the page. The kind of Writer who has, for as long as they can remember, adored writing and knew it was all they ever wanted to do[1]. This type of Writer is constantly juggling projects, some they'll finish and others they'll abandon. They hear a name on the street and think, "what a great name for an antagonist." They feel a jolt of both wonder and jealousy when reading something truly great, as they know that they've never read anything like it, but can never write anything quite like it either.

Then there is the Writer who desperately needs a minimum of six hundred dollars.

---

[1] But avoided saying so, because of how trite that sentiment is.

2

There are many who believe that these two types of Writer can, under the right circumstances, be one in the same. This is, however, not the case (as shown in the Venn diagram below). You cannot be both a romantic creative type with lofty dreams of writing the great American novel, or the next *Goodfellas*, while also longing for the feeling of six[2] to six hundred[3] green pieces of paper in your hand. These are mutually exclusive feelings. No one ever made six hundred dollars doing what they loved and if anyone tells you they did, return any purchased goods and run, because they are – and this isn't an exaggeration – going to kill you the first chance they get. The desperate dreamer is not to be trusted and will sooner resort to violence than art. This is perhaps the most important advice I can give. But it is not the only advice.

---

[2] If they're hundreds.
[3] If they're singles.

Inspired Writers

Writers Who Need 600 Dollars

Within the real or digital pages of this small-but-powerful book, you will find advice on how to break free from the shackles of passion and create your own book that sells enough copies to make you at least six hundred dollars. This advice will be presented in five steps, each one separated into its own chapter for the sake of tidiness and the fact that this is simply how books are traditionally organized. It is imperative that you **READ THESE CHAPTERS IN ORDER**. This is not *Uncle John's Bathroom Reader*, nor is it the *Guinness Book of World Records*, where you can just flip around, willy-nilly, expecting to find valuable information[4].

This book is a map to success, the directions of which must be followed in order, lest you find yourself lost on the road to success. Did you notice I just used the word "success" twice in the same sentence?[5] If not, just stop reading now. You're not even worth it. Everyone else, start pricing out mid-tier TVs, because you're about to be able to afford one.

---

[4] Because of this, there are no page numbers. You shouldn't need them. If you absolutely need page numbers, I encourage you to write them in as you read.

[5] There are a few of these little trials sprinkled throughout this book. Email me all of the spelling and grammar errors you find and I will send you your score!

CHAPTER 1: PREPARATION

This will be both mentally and physically taxing. If it were easy to write a book that makes over five hundred and ninety nine bucks, then everyone would do it. In order to reach the six hundred dollar destination, one must be ready for a truly daunting journey. Preparing for such an endeavor is a tricky balancing act with two all-too-common paths to failure:

1) Rushing preparation, in a misbegotten attempt to strike six hundred dollars' worth of gold as quickly as possible, only to realize that you have no idea what you've gotten yourself into.

2) Obsessing over the book you're *going* to write, without ever actually writing the damn thing. Excessive preparation leads to procrastination. The following are proven ways in which one can prepare, not only to write the proverbial goose that lays the six hundred dollar egg, but to prepare for any major artistic undergoing with a strictly financial goal. It is not necessary to hit all of these. Does that make you more comfortable? I sure hope not, because it IS absolutely necessary to hit all of these and if the very idea of not doing so excited you in any way, it's probably best you give up now. Like everything else in this book, you need to do this stuff in order. Don't try to be cute, just follow the steps:

0.   Make a list of steps you should do in order to prepare to write your book. This one's going to be pretty easy, considering I ALREADY DID IT FOR YOU. Didn't you notice that weird indent preceding this new section of sentences? Were you confused that it was a zero instead of a one? Well, now you know, it is a zero because I took care of it. You paid money for this book

and it was, almost literally, the least I could do. You're welcome, by the way.

1.   Consider your motive: Why do you need six hundred dollars?

a.   Is it absolutely essential that you get this money? As an example, has a high ranking member of a cartel taken your kindhearted nitwit of a brother hostage, demanding a six hundred dollar ransom if you ever want to see him again? If this is the case, I have to be honest, what the fuck is wrong with you? A drug lord kidnapped your brother and you went on Amazon and bought the cheapest book on how to make six hundred bucks? I mean, I get that it's a pretty specific amount and it's weird that a published book coincidentally contains that very same figure in its title, but you should really put your device down and call the cops. No cops? Hmmm, I was afraid you'd say that. Read on I suppose.

b.   Maybe you merely *want* six hundred dollars, but you don't necessarily *need* it. If that's the case, perhaps this project isn't worth your time. There are plenty of other things you could be doing with your life. Do you seriously not need six hundred dollars, though? Must be nice, fucker.

2.   Draw up a game plan: No, not an actual game plan (see image below). If you knew how to do something like that, you could easily make over six hundred dollars coaching high school sports[6]. Literal game plans are for the idle rich. Your game plan is metaphorical, and you better be familiar with metaphors if you plan on selling this thing. Indeed, this game plan could also be

---

[6] Or *almost* six hundred dollars coaching middle school sports.

called a to-do list, but calling it a game plan is cool and invokes

sport, which makes it seem like writing is merit-based and not

having-an-older-relative-who-works-for-a-reputable-publisher-

based. So, yeah, make a game plan of things you have to get done

around the house before you write this thing. And be realistic with

yourself, okay? We both know you're not going to do the roof on your garage. You've been putting it off for three years already, so

quit entertaining the idea of doing it.

Blocked Sites

- ✖ pornhub.com
- ✖ xvideos.com
- ✖ xxxvideos.com
- ✖ xxxxxxxxxvideos.com
- ✖ fucking.org
- ✖ thescenefromharoldandkumar.net
- ✖ bing.com/images
- ✖ whitehouse.com
- ✖ sickosexfreakgrossout.com
- ✖ cum.com
- ✖ com.cum
- ✖ cumcom.biz
- ✖ myspace.com/misstila
- ✖ youtube.com
- ✖ putlockers.me/movie/american-pie-3-american-wedding-207.html
- ✖ nudity.com
- ✖ daphnefakes.com
- ✖ velmafakes.com
- ✖ freddyfakes.com
- ✖ scooby-doo.net/forum/art

3. Install a browser add-on that blocks certain websites

and put every porn site you know into this thing: Hell, put the ones

you *don't* know into it. Add any other distractions that aren't

technically porn, but still give you orgasms. Now set the password

for the program to something like:

aposdijfpaoijpw43494393049uw0qjedpflkajsdojq409 and save it.

Bam, your computer is now useless for everything that isn't

writing. NOTE: You do not get to have "one for the road". While

allowing yourself one last hoorah before you hang it up and

become a full-time Writer may be a comforting notion, the very

idea of "one last big score" is harmful to anyone hoping to

accomplish any meaningful task. It is the cardinal procrastination.

You'll dangle this carrot in front of yourself for weeks, never truly

allowing yourself to block the evil, evil porn from your personal six-

hundred-dollar-printing money press.

4.   Assemble your Writing playlist: If you don't listen to

music, I *guess* that's fine. If you're a normal person, though,

you're gonna want to go with something simple that won't

distract you or excite you in any meaningful way. A lot of people

go with classical or jazz for this very reason, but I find classical to

be too recognizable and jazz to be too engaging[7]. I always use the

original motion picture soundtrack for movies I've never seen. No

---

[7] I am very smart and complex, you see.

chance of something being recognizable and very little chance of

any of it resonating with me one iota. For example, I am currently

listening to Brian Tyler's soundtrack for the Benicio del

Toro/Tommy Lee Jones vehicle *The Hunted*. It sucks. It's perfect.

5.   Make a small eight by ten frame: I

recommend using oak or cherry for this. Tape measure,

carpenter's pencil, small coping small, the works. You'll

figure it out. Stain the frame a respectable color and hang it on your wall. This is what we in the book writing biz like to call motivation. How is this going to motivate you? Well, imagine yourself fanning out six hundred dollars cash. You're wearing sunglasses and your favorite t shirt with the shark on it, and you look cool as hell and supremely content. Now imagine there is an eight by ten photograph of that image in a frame on your wall. Make the fucking frame.

 6. Cancel your plans with Catherine: Yes, she's nice, no one said she wasn't nice. You just don't really have time for the Catherines of the world right now. Can hanging out with a good friend be a healthy distraction from writing, so long as it isn't constantly dragging you away from the page? Yes, of course. But is Catherine really a *good* friend? I NEVER SAID CATHERINE WASN'T NICE. Anyways, yeah, tell her you have the flu or some shit. She'll forgive you, she's too nice not to.

7. Buy groceries: This is a lot like number 3. Having an errand to run is a surefire way to talk yourself out of writing, so the most effective way to combat this form of procrastination is to prevent it from happening. You're a grown up, so go to the grocery store, grab a cart, and stock up. You're going to do this thing in your brain, while writing, where you pretend you crave certain foods that you cannot possibly make without a trip to the store. The only way to be completely sure this will not occur is to get a little bit of everything. Will this be expensive? Sure, but we all know it takes money to make money, plus you probably *will* want banana bread in the future and bananas keep up to ten years in the freezer! Don't look it up. You know what, use that program to block google too. At least until you're done reading this book.

8. Make your Writer's Shirt: Every Writer wears their own Writer's Shirt, but what most people don't tell you is that it can be any color you want. Did most of the greats go with puffy paints or fabric markers on plain white Ts? Of course they did, it's a classic look. Still, that doesn't mean you can't separate yourself from the pack. Hell, a black V-neck and whiteout will do in a pinch. The important thing is that you have the shirt, it says the word Writer on it with an exclamation point, and you've drawn a portrait of yourself on the chest to the best of your ability. Mine looks like this:

Now that you've completed these steps, you're ready to start writing. If you haven't completed the steps, but you continued reading anyway, I genuinely don't care if you die tonight. I mean, I'm not going to actively root for it, but it seriously wouldn't phase me one bit.

Rot in hell.

CHAPTER 2: THE IDEA

The truth is, until you've written an entire book and profited a minimum of six hundred dollars from said book, you don't know shit. And what's that mean? It means your idea fucking sucks, bud. Hate to break it to you, but making money on non-fiction isn't going to happen[8]. It just isn't. If you want six hundred bucks, you have to use the Game of Thrones side of your brain where all of the cool stuff hangs out. And, within that section of your brain, there are some exploits you can implement in order to quickly come up with viable ideas for novels that will sell just enough copies to pass the six Benjamin mark. Surely you've heard variations of these or alternate ways to write

---

[8] Unless you're me or David McCullough

stories. Hell, there are many, many books and articles dedicated to giving the prospective Writer a leg up, but none of them promise you the untold riches that I've heralded on the cover of this book, have they?

Within each of these templates, I have included some examples, which are yours for the taking. Bear in mind, however, that other people are reading this book and can also use them, so it's sort of a race. GO!

COMBOS

Combos are fairly easy to get the hang of, as they involve merely combining two beloved properties in order to create your own story, making it *just* different enough that you don't owe anyone shit and you can take credit for the whole thing, with only a few rogue tweets about how you ripped off Tarantino or whatever.

1. ***Clerks + Taken = Closed for Lunch***: Okay, so by combining Kevin Smith's indie comedy classic *Clerks* with the massively successful Liam Neeson action vehicle *Taken*,

we have a guaranteed hit. Such a surefire smash, in fact,

that I'm tempted to quit writing this book and just do the

damn thing myself. We're talking upwards of three hundred

mil for this baby without breaking a sweat. Why? Think

about it. A trained killer whose girlfriend has sucked an

estimated 37 dicks? And he plays hockey on the roof and

then kills a guy with the stick? Oh, did you think these

Combos were going to be more subtle? Well, they're not.

Have you seen what Disney is doing lately? This shit is

incredibly easy and basic, just literally combine the stories.

The important thing here is that I picked *Taken* instead of

Die Hard to prove that I'm not a complete hack.

2.   ***Toy Story + Field of Dreams = Top of the***

Deck: Goddamn this is easy. Okay so you have an old man,

and his baseball cards come to life, and maybe some of

them get into the MLB and make a run for the World Series

or something. Then I guess the magic fades and the scrubs

on the bench have to seal the deal maybe... Look, I don't

have to write it, you do. Point is, this is a great idea and I

guarantee it will make two billion dollars in its first week at

the box office.

3.   ***Titanic + Rush Hour 2 = ???***: I'm going to level with you here. I got cocky and thought I could just combine the first two movies that came to my head and do a Combo and then say something like, "See how easy this is? I just thought of two movies completely at random and combined them for a summer blockbuster that, I shit you not, will cross the four billion mark by August." I cannot say that, though, because I cannot come up with a title. And without a title, there's no picture. I have, however, come up with a tagline for the thing and it's so good that it just might be enough to get the ball rollin: Laughter straight ahead. Gave myself chills with that one.

REVERSIES

Reversies are when you take the premise of an already popular story and reverse it. This is very, very easy to do, but very, VERY difficult to master. You probably shouldn't do it, honestly, but here are some examples.

1.   **Reverse *Happy Gilmore* = *Slummin' It*:** A professional golfer becomes fed up with the pretentiousness and classism of his chosen career and quits, instead joining a semi-professional hockey team where he excels because his naturally powerful drive has been converted into a deadly slap shot. Does he make it to the NHL? That's for you to decide, because I'm not writing this screenplay. I simply respect Tim Herlihy too much to bastardize his work in this text.

2.   **Reverse *Osmosis Jones* = *Reverse Osmosis***

Jones: Quite simply, the actor Bill Murray enters the body of

the cartoon Chris Rock. It's been a really long time since I

saw *Osmosis Jones* and, frankly, I thought it sucked ass. But

this title? Well, it's very funny and it came to me quickly

enough that I was as convinced of my genius as you, no

doubt, currently are. Still, this idea has legs and a gifted

Writer can spin this tale into gold like some sort of Reversies

Rumpelstiltskin. Which brings me to…

3.   **Reverse Rumpelstiltskin =**

Trimplerumpskin?: Okay, I'm embarrassed. I cannot, for the life of me, remember how that particular tale ends. I feel like the little fellow is somehow duped by a riddle and loses his powers and becomes a normal peasant or something? Or maybe he eats the poor lass and a valuable lesson is learned[9]? Either way, I'm not going to look it up because I feel like I've already proven my point, which is that this isn't as hard to do as I've led you to believe. It is borderline impossible to fail using this method. I wrote the map, but I can't drive you there too, know what I'm saying?

---

[9] Those stories were dark, so this is probably more likely.

Trimplerumpskin

8 HEADS IN A DUFFEL BAG

This tip is really tricky but, when executed correctly, yields undeniable results. Up to this point, only Tom Schulman has been able to successfully write *8 Heads in a Duffel Bag*, but I genuinely think there's room to not only learn from Schulman, but potentially surpass him, in terms of knocking out a quality story that follows the *8HiaDB* template. That being said, this is no easy undertaking. I have been trying to replicate the magic of *8 Heads* for the better part of a decade, to absolutely no avail. The main problem, I think, is that I have already seen the film and cannot hope to write without picturing and hearing Joe Pesci's voice. Sometimes having a specific actor or person in mind for a character can be great for finding that character's voice. Such is not the case when you are trying to recreate something that already exists and have it be something other than a Van Santian carbon copy. So, should you choose this method, make sure that you have never seen *8HiaDB* and, for the love of god, bring extra coffee!!!

OTHER

Please, allow me to let out the longest, most aggressive sigh of all time. Alright, go ahead and lay it on me. Tell me about how you're special and you have "so many ideas" and you don't need me holding your hand on this thing. Right, you just bought a book on writing, but you're an expert, I hear ya. Okay genius, go ahead and try me. If your brilliant, original idea checks all (ALL) of the following boxes, I take back everything I'm about to say. If, however, it checks none or only *some* of the boxes, then remove your shirt. You are no Writer.

- **The protagonist gets the band back together**

So important, this. *Italian Job*, the *Mighty Ducks* sequels, *Ocean's Eleven*, the GOOD stuff. Every truly memorable story has a part toward the end of act one where the protagonist collects their friends. This is great for two reasons. 1) It introduces us to all of the characters quickly and efficiently. 2) I like it. Yes, I am such a fan of this type of moment in storytelling that, when tasked with writing my own Dogme 95 style manifesto in a film class, I wrote about this type of scene and my love of Puerto Rican character actor Luis Guzman. And, unfortunately, you can't really include Luis Guzman in your story, except...

- **Include Luis Guzman in your story**

Yeah, so I haven't really changed all that much over the six-or-so years since taking that class. That was a manifesto, which I took to mean that, were I to commit a very serious crime, these were the thoughts I would be remembered for. And I can think of no better idea to include in such a document than watching Seth Green invent Napster in *Italian Job* or watching Guzman act circles around everyone in his vicinity in the shockingly high volume of classics he has appeared in. NOTE: Go ahead and take a look at the filmography of Mr. Guzman. Soderbergh, De Palma, Paul Thomas Anderson, I do not have to continue. He is a consummate professional and he has been married to the same woman since 1985 despite the fact that he is AN

34

ACTOR. So, yes, I DO expect you to include him in your story,

even if it's something as simple as having a character say,

"Did you see that new movie with Luis Guzman? The best!"

- **Subvert Chekhov's Gun**

Duhhhhh the gun should go off later if you show it duhhhhhhh DOOOIIIIIII. Who cares? Look, I've seen some guns in my day and they don't always go off. That's just the way it is. It can be fun to do variations on Chekhov's Gun, such as Chekhov's bear trap (*Straw Dogs*) or Chekhov's awkward sexual encounter (*Superbad*), but it's more fun to just completely drop plot elements and leave the audience wanting more. Furthermore, if you want to have a bloody shootout at the end of your story, don't worry about showing the gun up front. Foreshadowing is cool if you're in seventh grade, but a surprise bloody shootout? That's the Writer's dream, baby!

- **NO SEX SCENES**

Yuck! No way, José, do I want to read some sweaty, pornographic paragraph about how someone "unsheathed" or "thrusted" this or that. That ain't what the Roc-man[10]

---

[10] I sometimes call myself the Roc-man.

comes to fiction for. There is unfortunately no way to write

a sex scene that is actually sexy. They are either funny,

gross, or both. That's it. So, unless you want to write

something funny or gross, steer clear from the bedroom, or

any other room you plan on having people get down to

business in. If you absolutely *have* to, just write, like, "they

boned" or something. We'll get the idea.

CHAPTER 3: SPLIT DECISIONS

On April 4th, 2012 the massively popular CBS procedural CSI: Crime Scene Investigation made, quite possibly, the most groundbreaking single episode of television in the history of the medium: "Split Decisions". This entire chapter is about that episode.

If you have never seen an episode of CSI or any of its spinoffs before, don't worry. I mean, maybe see a doctor and rule out the possibility that you're not even alive, but other than that, it's not a big deal if you've never caught an episode. The legitimacy of "Split Decisions" does not require you to have even a passing knowledge of the show or its characters. Do pay attention, though, because it's a fuckin' doozie.

The episode starts, as all CSI episodes do, with a cold open. On the floor of a casino, an obese smoker with an oxygen tank (Cheryl Hawker) hits a modest jackpot on a slot machine and, as the machine's bell goes off, a middle-aged man (Vaugh Armstrong) is shot in the stomach by a younger gentleman (Joshua Desroches). The casino goes into lockdown, with the CSIs and police officers frantically searching the place for the assailant, as Archie (Archie Kao) uses the casino's "eye in the sky" camera system to scan for signs of the suspect. His tech quickly picks up a "ninety seven percent" match and he calls out the suspect's location, but before the agents can apprehend the perpetrator, he has seemingly vanished. Moments later, Archie once again gets a hit, sending an agent to a completely different area in the casino, again to no avail. After a third sighting and a third near-miss, the officers realize that the stairwell door wasn't properly locked and the killer could be anywhere in the hotel or casino, with a gun. "So how the hell'd he get away?" a befuddled

Nick Stokes (George Eads) asks. The Who's smash 1978 hit "Who

Are You?" plays.

We come back from commercial and learn from DB

Russell (Ted Danson) that the victim was "a doctor with a

family," before Julie Finlay (Elisabeth Shue) reenacts the crime

and finds another bullet in a nearby slot machine.

Credits still on the screen, we cut back to Stokes and

Morgan Brody (Elisabeth Harnois) who, while looking for the

suspect, encounter a scantily clad woman who boned him the

night before. She "kinda made a video" and the suspect (calling

himself "X Man") left behind some DNA, if ya know what I mean!

We cut to Sarah Sidle (Jorja Fox) and Jim Brass (Paul

Guilfoyle) who are searching the victim's hotel room and I shit

you not, the credits are still fucking going! Anyway, they find the

victim's son, Avery (Jackson Pace), playing XBox and living it up in

the hotel room. While Avery learns of his father's murder, we

learn from Avery that his mother died last year. They came out

to Vegas to see a Kanye West concert and his dad won eight

hundred dollars on a slot machine, which Avery assumes

prompted his murder. The opening credits mercifully end here,

as Avery shares how much of a spoiled little shit he is and

humble brags about his new pair of busted ass Reebok Zigs.

We return to Stokes and Brody, who are searching

another hotel room – this one inhabited by some paranoid

douchebag with small feet (Christopher Maxwell). The guy's

obvious guilt alerts the two CSIs to the fact that his roommate is the suspect, which is confirmed when they find the killer[11] hiding in the closet. They take him back to the station, where he tells them his name is Jordan Brentson (Desroches again) and he's adamant that the man in the photo, who committed the act, isn't actually him. He claims to have come to Vegas after winning the trip in some sort of contest. Stokes isn't having it, since he knows they found his blood and DNA in all the places the suspect has been linked to. Brody meets with Archie, who confirms both the suspect's alibi and what the CSIs think occurred. "How can a guy be in two places at the same time?" Archie asks in the most cliché way you can possibly imagine. "He can't," Brody frustratedly responds. Commercial.

We're back, with Brody telling Russell and some others that their suspect is *not* a twin, much to their dismay. It isn't all bad news, though, as she links the actual killer to an ATM and discovers his name is Xavier Marx (Desroches yet again). Sidle, Stokes, and the cops go to Marx's hotel room, where he's boning some hot twins with bad line deliveries and here I am thinking

---

[11] Or who they assume is the killer at that time.

I'm suddenly watching a goddamn Coors Light commercial! They take Marx back to the station where he reveals that he, too, "won a free trip."

The CSIs are in the lab, wondering just how these two could possibly look so much alike despite not being twins[12]. One of them supposes they could have faked the birth records somehow, but they're still unable to nail the suspect, since, as Russell notes, they have, "identical DNA. No way to prove which one pulled the trigger." Except Finlay has a trick up her sleeve: Antibody profiling. We go to the lab and hear – and this isn't an exaggeration, I can assure you – the most laborious exposition of all time. Then we get the radical Bruckheimer montage of all sorts of wacky tubes and computers and shit and BAM. No match for either one of them. Commercial. We're only halfway through this thing, baby!

We return again, with the CSIs in the middle of a discussion about in vitro fertilization, with Russell explaining that frozen embryos are, "the only way you can get identical triplets,

---

[12] I'm going to keep calling them twins, by the way. It's just so much easier.

from one set of parents, born of three different families." Then he gets an alert. Brentson's lawyer showed up and it's also his mother (Stepfanie Kramer). They throw their miracle baby theory at her and she becomes emotional, revealing that she could only care for the one child and has never seen or met the others. Brass thinks she's in on it. But, as most of us know, Brass ain't always right.

In the ballistics lab, Finlay discovers that the type of bullet used in the murder is commonly used by air marshals. Brody, meanwhile, checks with the hotel to see if there was, in fact, a contest for a free trip to Vegas. There was, but it was clearly created by the twins because, hey wait a second they're not twins they're triplets! That's right, the air marshal is the third doppelganger, Kevin Chance (Desroches, duh), and now the primary suspect and THIS EPISODE IS VERY WORTHWHILE. When they go to Chance's room, they find him long dead of an apparent overdose, murder weapon in the room. They also find a confession he recorded on his laptop, where he reveals that Dr. Kiel's attempt to play god is what drove him to commit the crime and take his own life. Sidle asks Stokes if he thinks this is the answer they've been looking for. "We've been chasing the wrong guy this whole time," he says, "Why should we have the right one now?" Pretty badass. Commercial.

Back at the autopsy lab with Russell and fan favorite Dr.

Robbins (Robert David Hall), we learn that the video wasn't

exactly as it appeared to be. Turns out Chance suffered some

blunt force trauma to the head and was force fed drugged

scotch, meaning one of the other twins faked the video as well.

Which is why Russell delivers the very sick line, "I smell the twins at work here." Brody and Stokes, meanwhile, learn that Dr. Kiel

is the one that booked the trips for the triplets, but why? Two

days before he was murdered he withdrew one hundred and

fifty thousand dollars, possibly to pay the triplets off. Then Finlay

learns that the antibody profiling on the scotch bottle rules all

three of the lookalikes out. A fourth one? You're darn tootin'!

Sidle goes to Kiel's room to talk to Avery and see if he knows anything about the trip or the plot to kill his dad and Chance. He tells her he saw those men with his dad and is upset when Sidle reminds him that he'll be staying with his family in Wisconsin. She kindly takes him downstairs for some ice cream to make him feel better. Stokes goes back to Archie at the eye in the sky camera and he gets another hit. They call Sidle to tell her and she asks where the suspect is. "Right behind you," Stokes says. It's the kid!!!! The kid is also one of the other guys and he's a super villain!

Back at the station we discover that this kid's a fuckin' crook. He spent a bunch of his dad's money and, when Brass reveals that Avery is the sole beneficiary in Kiel's will, the kid plays dumb. But they also know that he set up payments to be made to the other brothers, minus Chance who Avery seemingly set up. But, like he says, they all have the same DNA, so it's hard to prove who did any of it. "There was some bad seed in that petri dish," Brass says, in a line the episode was probably written around. Then Avery talks about how his mom couldn't get pregnant and how his whole life is a lie. He decides to take his chances in court and the episode ends. I shit you not. That's how they chose to end this episode.

Now, if you're less wise than a real Writer, you're still wondering: Why, in this book about how to write a book that makes at least six hundred dollars, did I just read one thousand six hundred and twenty six words on a Danson-era CSI episode? Granted, this question does have a degree of validity, mostly because post-Grissom CSI is notoriously weak compared to the early years. *However*, I believe the answer is more than obvious. I have included a chapter about Split Decisions because it proves, unequivocally, that you can make money writing about literally anything.

Doubters will, perhaps even rightly, compare this chapter to the whaling section of Moby Dick. They would, of course, be missing the point, just as they were with Melville's undeniable classic. Genuine Dickheads[13] know that the information about whaling is *essential* to the novel, just as an understanding and appreciation of season 12, episode 19 of CSI is essential not only to the understanding of *this* book, but to making six hundred dollars writing a book of your own.

We're far enough into this that I can start to really level with you. My advice, though near-essential, is still just that. Advice. And there are obvious exceptions to the many important rules that I have included in these pages. Season 12, episode 19 of CSI just happens to be the most obvious of those exceptions. It is, very simply put, the dumbest fucking thing I have ever seen. It is so aggressively stupid that I had to immediately watch it again as soon as it ended, watching it a third time (while showing it to my wife) the very next day. I have also watched it a fourth and fifth time in writing this chapter. When you've seen "Split Decisions" as much as I have, it becomes quite clear how it was written. Whenever the episode's story reaches a decision or a fork in the road, as it were, the Writers have chosen the worst of

---

[13] What ride or die Moby Dick fans call themselves.

the two (or more) options. The eye in the sky gets an immediate hit on the suspect? The suspect is gone. Oh, they found him? Well, that's actually not him, it's just a guy who looks exactly like him. Oh, they found the identical other guy? Well, uhh, that's not him either. You get the idea.

For it to culminate with the single most ludicrous conclusion in television history[14] only makes logical sense if you've seen the episode. In fact, the episode is so ludicrous that I PREDICTED THE ENDING HALFWAY THROUGH. That should have been impossible, since the ending is, on paper, completely out of the question for a way to end something. Take, as a comparison, the movie *Saw*. *Saw* has a great twist that no one saw coming, because it was impossible to see coming unless you were being a dick. I know that because I, myself, guessed who the killer was and I was absolutely, actively being an asshole, which my friends made sure to let me know once the movie ended. Now, imagine the movie *Saw* is as over-the-top outrageous as Split Decisions.

---

[14] Obviously there will be those who think that the end of Lost or The Sopranos is worse, which I would grant you if context mattered. But context doesn't matter.

There are four different Danny Glovers and one of them is a child and they all get together to frame Jigsaw for a series of grisly murders in order to procure a pair of sneakers and a ticket to a Yeezy show. You'd maybe be more likely, in that situation, to realize that, yes, one of the Danny Glovers is white and he's on the floor and he's shocking the Australian guy from the Insidious movies.

My point is this: None of this matters if you have an audience. People are very, very stupid and will watch or read nearly anything, so long as it is competently written and they *think* it has value[15]. But how do you trick someone into thinking that your maybe-shitty story has value? Well, I thought you'd never ask!

---

[15] Please don't read any deeper into this until you're done with my book and have forgotten about it.

CHAPTER 4: Cellar Door

You feel that? That tingling on your neck? Why, that's

because "cellar door" is the most pleasant sounding combination

of sounds in the English language of course. After all, the Lord of

The Lord of the Rings said it, so it must be true! Well, it isn't true

and he's not even the original person who said it[16]. No, the

combination of phonemes that are the most pleasing to the ear

isn't "cellar door". It's "seller door"[17]. This is, of course, the

metaphorical door that you step through when you go from an

everyday chump to a bona fide book seller. And Tolkien would

---

[16] The true originator of this theory is, according to the New York Times at the time I'm writing this book, unknown.

[17] The chapter is called Cellar Door, because that was the only way to make the reveal affective. If I would have just called it "Seller Door" you would have seen it coming from a mile away.

have known that if he understood metaphors instead of playing make-em-ups all the livelong day and inventing modern fantasy.

So, how does one cross through that wonderful seller door, and into the comfortable home of money and expensive hobbies? Here's where most Writers would tell you something like, "it's going to take a lot of hard work and discipline, but if you put your mind to it, bust your butt every day, and follow my five simple steps, there's nothing you won't be able to achieve." I'm not going to say that, though, because it isn't a lot of hard work. It's super fucking easy. Almost anyone can do it and I can't believe more people don't know how to get the job done. I suspect, though, that the reason they don't know how to get the job done is because they haven't followed my five simple steps, which I will now lay out for you.

How to Write a Book

&

Make At Least

Six Hundred Dollars.

By: Rocco Tenaglia

1. **Make sure the cover is bangin'**: They say don't judge a book by its cover, but the idiom wouldn't exist if people didn't definitely, always, one hundred percent judge books by their covers. With digital copies, it's even more likely to hook the would-be-reader. Make sure that thumbnail is on point, because if it's trash they're gonna scroll right on by. For this, I recommend turning to a trusted friend who knows how to draw and blackmailing or bribing them for their work[18]. After all, if you pay someone for services rendered then that counts against the six hundred dollars. Now you have to make, I don't know, like six hundred and forty dollars or something for it to actually count. Anyway, I recommend just making it look vaguely like a very popular book that already exists, using the knockoff video game console method that beguiles unsuspecting grandparents during the holidays. Also, make sure you get some sort of explicit tag somewhere because swearing is cool and so is violence. No one will read the book if they

---

[18] If they *already* owe you one, even better.

think it's bereft of the two. I choose to include parental advisory stickers on my books to really drive this point home: this book is fuckin' cool.

2.   **Gotta have a pull-quote!**: This is a must. And I'm not talking about the ironic pull-quote where you find a review from some big critic who read the book and put that on the cover to Eminem-at-the-end-*of-8-Mile* any negative opinion someone should have about it. That style of pull-quote had already fallen out of fashion the third time someone did it. Nor am I referring to the kind where you find some random guy named Barock Obamma in an attempt to deceive the dyslexic. I mean an honest-to-god pull-quote from a legit celebrity. You're never going to get them to actually read your book, but that doesn't matter. Just ask them to write a pull-quote on a social media site of your choosing and, if they respect Writing, they'll do it. If, for some reason, you don't get any takers and grow impatient, you can just lie! Seriously, it's parody law or

something. Perfectly legal. Just write whatever you want and attribute it to a very famous person. Think about it. Does Katy Perry really have time to take some struggling writer to court over this sort of thing? She absolutely does not. Plus she'd look like a total asshole, even though you're clearly the one in the wrong!

3.   **The price has to be right:** This one's big. Charge too much and you could scare people off. Charge too little and people will assume your work is worthless. Truly a conundrum. Oh, wait a second; it's actually not at all a conundrum. Charge two bucks! Yes, everything that is for sale should cost two dollars[19]. It is the best price there is. If everything was two dollars, well, I'd own everything. And I'd still have scratch to spare. If you're too thick to process this, please see the graph below.

---

[19] Or five dollars. It felt unfair not to include five dollars as an amount some things should cost. It's a good amount.

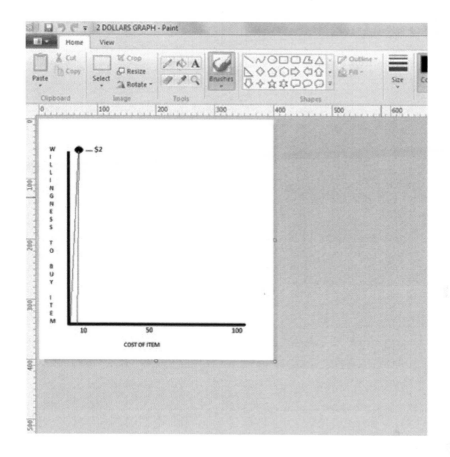

4.   **Marketing:** I know nothing about marketing, but it seems that having a good story to go with the product often works, especially with art. People like getting something and also feeling good about themselves for a good deed. It helps them justify irresponsible purchases

which, face it, your book[20] will probably be. For example, I

wrote this book to pay off hospital bills when my wife was

sick. Don't steal that either, because that's good shit. Did

you know my wife was sick when you bought this book?

Well, it's true, she was and I'm a hero. If you didn't know

that, though, then why did you buy this book? See numbers

1-3, pal! Anyway, I'm not going to tell you to lie for this one,

because that would make you a reprehensible fuck. But,

honestly, if there wasn't something legitimate driving you to

write this book, then there's really no reason to write the

book. I'm sure you'll come up with something appropriately

sympathy-inducing. Once you have, make sure you work it

into that dedication page you always see right before the

book actually starts. You can learn a lot from a Writer by

how classy their dedications are. For example, all-time great

rap music writer Biggie Smalls dedicated his album *Ready to*

Die to all the teachers that told him he'd never amount to

---

[20] This is not a slight against you. It is true of all books except for books on how to learn magic and the Prima strategy guide for the N64 game *Banjo Tooie*, which I consider to be an invaluable text.

anything, all of the people that lived above the buildings that he was hustling in front of who called the police on him when he was just trying to make some money to feed his daughter, *and* all of his peoples in the struggle. He even told them it was all good baby baybayyy. Now *that's* class.

5.   **About the author**: In the old days, the about the author would go either in the back or on the back and would detail the career of the person who wrote the book (aka the Writer). Now, with eBooks, you find them in the preview images of the products. This really hammers home the entire point of the "about the author" page: it is there to move units. Yes, you use this page to try and coax the reader into purchasing the book they're considering getting. This is why it is imperative that you nail it. And, rather than tell you exactly how to do that, I'm just going to show you.

(YOUR FACE[21] HERE)

ABOUT THE AUTHOR ←(INEXPLICABLY DIFFERENT FONT/SIZE.

UNDERLINE IT)

(YOUR NAME) is a brilliant writer hailing from (WHERE YOU'RE

FROM). His/Her/Their previous work includes (STUFF YOU

WROTE. MAKE SOMETHING UP IF YOU HAVE TO TO PROVE YOU

ARE SUCCESFUL). He/She/They enjoy(s) philosophy, fly fishing,

and yoga and currently resides in (A REALLY EXPENSIVE

NEIGHBORHOOD YOU WILL NEVER LIVE IN) with his/her/their

(EXOTIC PET) (NAME OF EXOTIC PET).

---

[21] Bonus if you're very good looking.

Publishing

So, with the five simple steps out of the way, you still have a big decision to make. Do you sell this as a physical book or as a digital download on the Amazon store? This, unlike previous steps in the chapter, *is* in fact a conundrum. And that's why it's not numbered and the word "publishing" is centered. It's too important.

The obvious choice here is, of course, to go the tried and true route: A good old fashioned physical copy. After all, no one ever brags about their very good plus condition first edition of the *Catcher in the Rye* eBook they downloaded from Amazon, and for good reason. The true brainiacs will often talk about the weight of the book, the feeling of turning the page, of seeing your progression through a story readily and tangibly. Even bigger dorks and dweebs will cite the smell of the pages, the glue, the dust[22]. To tell you the truth, though, none of that stuff

---

[22] The idea of being excited over tiny pieces of dead skin that prove you are a messy person is quite the head-scratcher, I must say.

actually matters. There is one – and only one – real reason to publish your book this way: You can charge more for it.

Yes, people are willing to fork over more of their hard earned cash if you actually hand them something they can hold. It's just the way it is. They're also more comfortable spending more on something they can loan to a friend and don't have to worry about disappearing off of their device of choice, should the company they bought it from go under. People also love signed versions of things, and you can't sign an eBook[23].

But physical copies mean higher publishing costs. Yes, the sad truth is if you plan on peddling your wears in the real world, you have to put up some of that money that you so desperately need. If you're the gambling type, this will be quite the thrill. Remember, the goal isn't to simply receive six hundred dollars, it is to *profit* that amount. And, after the tremendous cost of

---

[23] Another weird one. Autographs with dedications kill resale value, even though the autographed product almost always costs substantially more than the clean, unvandalized version. Because of this, I have decided to charge one dollar *less* for any copy of this book. If you already bought the book, unsigned, mail it to me and I will sign it and send it back, along with one dollar.

publishing x copies of your book, six hundred bucks total would be a colossal failure.

Publishing the book electronically, while unglamorous, could be the better route. First, it costs almost nothing, other than the colossal pain in the ass that will be caused by dealing with formatting and converting your manuscript to the appropriate file type for Amazon's eBook store. Bear in mind, though, that the people who write books about dinosaurs fucking the tailpipes of 2007 Chevy Silverados have figured this part of it out, so you should be fine. Easier still is the speed of publishing electronically. You don't have to worry about finding a printer and waiting for the copies of the book to be complete, nor would you have to stress about the actual stocking and selling of the book. It's just on amazon. Shoot your aunt a link. She'll buy two!

Unfortunately, though – and this may be the most important thing, so I'll reiterate it here – you cannot sign an eBook. Now, I know I'm currently a nobody. Who am I to deface a copy of this excellent book with my shittily written name and maybe a drawing of a shark or a silly face or something? Well, I agree, and that is why if *I* sign a copy of this book, I will give the person receiving the signature a dollar. I respect the art form too much not to. But this doesn't mean that is always the case. No, by the time my next book rolls around, I fully expect this Rocco Tenaglia[24] to be worth roughly twice the cost of the book itself! And what better way to make in-roads with the physical copy people than to publish a damn physical copy of *this* book?

I'm not going to tell you how to do this part. I genuinely think it's somewhat of a toss-up. But, if you're confident with the product you're putting out, I would highly recommend doing both. That's what Paul Giamatti and Melanie Lynskey like to call a win/win! Appeasing both the tech-savvy, hard-on-cash, Writers to be and the know-it-all, bookworm, rat bastard purists – not to mention the various family members who'll be asking for a copy and don't know how to access their own email, let alone

---

[24] I fully expect this to become an alternate to John Hancock and, to be honest, I think it sounds a lot better.

purchase and read an eBook. Indeed, this is the best way. But as long as you're making your hard work available in one way or another, there are no wrong answers.

The people thirst for sweet elixir that is your book. Quench their thirst[25].

---

[25] This is as close to writing a sex scene as I'll ever get, by the way.

CHAPTER 4.5 (THE *REAL* CHAPTER 5): YOU DID IT!

As soon as I started writing this book, I had this terrible

pit in my stomach. I kept wondering, 'What about the good for

nothing hacks who skip right to the last chapter, in hopes of finding the pot of gold without riding the Writing rainbow? What about those fucks?' And that thought plagued my beautiful brain for three entire days, until I had an idea. An awful idea. Like the Grinch before me, I had a wonderful, awful idea.

'They'll start flipping through pages from the back,' I thought, 'oh, I do hate those hack fucks. I hate them a lot!'

'It won't end with chapter five,' I cried, with a laugh. 'Why, I'll end it on chapter four and a half!'

So I laid out the book, there on Microsoft Word, typing up first chapter, second, then third. And when it came time for the last to arrive, I simply typed out CHAPTER 4.5. Leaving 5 for those whom I wish weren't alive.

And Rocco himself carved the roast beast.

So, yeah, this is the real chapter 5 and chapter 5 will be a full-on decoy, littered with terrible advice that I guarantee will prevent any would-be Writer from ever seeing even a fraction of six hundred dollars. In fact, I'm going to call them "writers" and not even capitalize the W, which is *always* capitalized when speaking of a true Writer[26]. And if you skipped ahead and you're reading this now, congratulations, you made it to the good stuff; the primo Writing tips. You betrayed my trust and I have no choice but to reward you for it with great advice. SERIOUSLY AWESOME MAN, GREAT JOB[27]!

Now that *that's* out of the way, and I know you're on the level when it comes to reading in order, we can get to the good stuff. You've written a book and – assuming you've followed at least the majority of my direction – made at least six hundred dollars. Look at your hands. Notice anything different? No? Well you should, because they're no longer normal hands. They are now the hands of a Writer and a damned good one. Still, I'd have to imagine you're scratching your head and thinking, "Well I've accomplished my main goal in life, but *now* what?" Well I'm not going to come out and say that's a stupid question, but it's not a great one, bud. There is, as is often the case in writing, only one logical next step: spend that mother fucking money.

---

[26] Sometimes it is even spelled Writor, but only for the very good ones.
[27] You're a fucking piece of shit.

Why, after pouring your heart and soul into your work for

all this time, would you want your six hundred dollar prize to rot

away in some stingy bank vault next to Buffet[28] and Bezos'

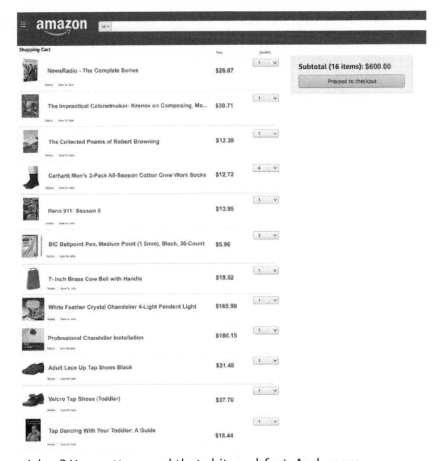

riches? You gotta spend that shit, and *fast*. And, more

specifically, you have to spend it on these exact things.

---

[28] No extra t necessary. I am speaking, of course, of the immortal, tropical bard Jimmy Buffet.

1. **Ben & Jerry's Half Baked (one pint) - $5**: Diet be damned, you earned this tasty treat. Honestly, what better way to celebrate a job well done than with sixteen ounces of brownie, cookie dough, vanilla goodness? I'm honestly asking. Do you know a better way to celebrate a job well done? Well, I do, and it's

2. **Glenkinchie 12 Year (750 ml) - $60**: This is, in fact, exactly what daddy likes. And I am daddy in this particular scenario. Simply put, this is the best scotch I've ever had that didn't cost twenty percent of what this book will be netting you. Any serious Writer needs to at least attempt to develop a taste for mid-level scotch, so as to fit in. Buy it. Drink it. Enjoy it[29].

3. **Kyrie 4 Halloweens (Size 11) - $150**: Who doesn't love a great pair of sneakers? And, while you don't necessarily want to break the bank here (see above), you can't really skimp if you want to be treated with any semblance of respect from the sneakerhead community

---

[29]RESPONSIBLY.

(and trust me, you DO[30]). So, while the Halloweens aren't the most desirable Nike out there, they're still plenty respectable and plenty badass. Google them suckers. All black with the green slime from Ninja Turtles splattered all over the greatest logo in history. Love that Kyrie 4 silhouette. Trust me, you need these shoes.

4.   **Get a damn car wash (with under wash) - $8**: They say you're supposed to wash your vehicle once every two weeks, but that's poppycock. You can easily go months on end without visiting a car wash, unless you're one of those off-roading types and I happen to know for a fact you aren't because you are attempting to write a book. They also say not to spring for the under wash unless you live in an area where salt is used when it snows. That's probably true, but I have no idea. I'm not a car underbody scientist, I'm a Writer. I say get the under wash regardless. It's only like a dollar extra and buddy... You can afford it! Despite

---

[30] They are a famously level-headed and kind group, whose respect – once earned – could change your life.

what some of the experts say, one thing is absolutely agreed

on: car washes are fun! Being sensually come-hithered into

the tracks, sprayed with rainbow water, and slapped around

by the big spinny things? It's a hoot and a holler and the

fourth thing you should spend your book money on. Tip the

toweler[31]!

5. **KitchenAid Stand Mixer - $350**: Look, your

Zucchinana bread™[32] is good, but it isn't perfect. And maybe

that's because you're still hand mixing it like some lowly

Dark Age peasant. To be fair to the peasants of old, there is

honor in hard work. There just ain't good food in hard work,

unless you want to spend all day contracting Carpal Tunnel.

And yes, I'm well aware that this is more than half of what

you hope and expect to make on this project. If you already

have one, you can spend this money on number 7. But – and

be honest here – do you already have one? Yeah, I didn't

think so, bitch. Wrack 'em.

---

[31] Sometimes there are two towelers. And, while I don't agree with this practice, it is imperative that you tip both of them. You can afford it, so don't be a dick.
[32] Formerly bananachini bread

6.   My next book - $5: I mean, you've read this much right? Clearly you adore my way with words or, at the very least, feel as though you have learned from them. When you think about it logically, buying my next book makes more sense than maybe any other purchase on this list. Plus, get a good look at that price tag. I feel like I've earned that three dollar bump and the fact that you made it this far absolutely supports that. Oh, virtual shop keep! I'll take two!

7.   Your wife's hospital bills - $2600: Again, I'm not some dullard. I can absolutely see that this is a fair amount more than what this book will most likely be netting you in the way of profit. But do I think you should rob yourself of number 1 through 5, simply because your sick wife had a few extended stays in the hospital that are costing your small family lots of money? Well, that question has two answers 1) The Kyrie 4 has an unparalleled silhouette, even compared to the Jordan XIII. 2) Medical bills have no interest, so who gives a shit. At the end of the day, follow your bliss. The insurance industry has us all by the balls. Don't bend to their every whim. Treat yourself.

NOTE: YOU MIGHT[33] MAKE MORE THAN SIX HUNDRED DOLLARS

I'm sure you thought I'd never get to this and, to be honest, I never thought I'd get to it either. It's not that I don't have any faith in you, it's just that I don't have any faith in the system. The idea of any mortal making more than six hundred bucks off of words they wrote down that other people bought to read and learn from or be entertained by is a pretty ridiculous notion. I'm flummoxed by it, myself. Still, on the off chance that some unearthly miracle *does* happen to occur here and you *do* hit the big time, making seven, eight, perhaps *NINE* hundred dollars, I feel like I must dole out some last-minute advice. No fancy lists here, just one simple idea, followed by a brief paragraph

---

[33] This is in no way a guarantee and the author of this text is not responsible for showing the reader how to make *more* than six hundred dollars.

explaining why I chose to share that idea and ending with a sentence that leaves the reader thinking. Kid stuff.

Don't Let This Get To Your Head!

Stop me if you've heard this one before: Lowly would-be-Writer buys a how-to book, follows the steps, churns out a work of their own, and strikes it rich. The seven hundred dollar profit they've reaped goes straight to their head, they abandon their friends and loved ones, move to Los Angeles, develop a cocaine habit, murder a drifter, dispose of the body in the alley of a less popular night club, move back home, get a job at the mall, and have to start all over? Yes, this is a tale as old as tales themselves, but it's certainly an avoidable one.

When you set the lofty goal of earning six hundred dollars off of art, one penny more means you have achieved the impossible. And when people achieve the impossible, they begin to (perhaps even validly) feel like they are more than human. Gods, as it were. And when people think they are gods, they do irrational things. All of this to say: stay grounded. You are a human being. You cannot fly, you cannot read minds, and you cannot murder a drifter without it catching up to you. All you can do is read my book, write a book of your own, and then read my next book. In conclusion, buy my next book. The title is a secret but trust me, it's going to be a masterwork rivalling the best offerings from your favorite author[34]. You'll love it. And, if you read every word in the right order, who knows? That whole "human" thing we were talking about? Let's just say it doesn't *have* to be this way. ;)

---

[34] I don't know who your favorite author is, but this clever trick allows me to seem like I do!

CHAPTER 5: YOU DID IT!

Well, you made it! You finally read through the whole

book and now you're at chapter 5, the final chapter with all of

the secrets for what you *really* need to write a book that makes you at least six hundred dollars. Heh heh heh. Give yourself a pat on the back because you've earned it. But before we get into the trade secrets, how about a quick review of some of the most important lessons presented in chapters 1-4.

1.   **Never read ahead**: By now you're tired of hearing it, as it has been hammered home throughout these pages. People who read ahead are the kind of people who would gladly stab their closest friend in the eye with a mechanical pencil if it meant they had a better chance of winning the Powerball. These people are scum and that's all there is to it. A pox on them and theirs. May they never have children.

2.   **Always write everything in red pen:** I know, I know, you read the book and you're sick of me harping on you about the red pen thing, but it really works! When you write every single thing that comes to your mind longhand, in a grid-style notebook, with a red ballpoint pen, there is a guaranteed higher chance of landing six hundred singles.

And that's what you're here for, right? The secrets to the six hundred? Turns out you've been getting some of the best stuff along the way and the red pen thing, well, that's some of the best of the best.

3.   **Be sure to include recognizable characters:** You want people to read your book and one of the best ways to ensure that happens is to include characters the would-be-reader has already encountered in some of their favorite works of art! I recommend carefully picking and choosing from all sorts of media. A caped crusader here, a tragically romantic couple there. Maybe even a newscaster, just so long as whoever picks up the book can thumb through it and say, "Hey, I know that character! This book must be very good!" Hell, you might even want to include a certain cartoon swine and his iconic catchphrase to close the book out. Nothing wrong with that!

4.   **Don't eat while you're writing:** In chapter 4, we discussed the writing process in detail and, if you took

one thing from that section, I sincerely hope it was this: DO NOT EAT WHILE YOU ARE WRITING A BOOK. Not while you're physically writing, not while you're brainstorming ideas, not while you're taking a break. Never. From the time you come up with an idea for a book until the time you finish the final draft, you should not eat any food. This is because, as we've been over, eating makes you less likely to come up with great ideas. I don't need to revisit the science of it all, but when you're hungry you're running on pure adrenaline and that's when the best writing gets done. Haven't you ever heard someone say that of a great artist? "They were successful because they wanted it more than anyone else. They were hungry!" Well, this is what that meant!

5.   **Call your relatives and tell them about your book:** Many people are skeptical about this one, but it works. Calling many of your friends and family members to tell them about your project is a great way to motivate

yourself and get some free fans who will constantly ask you for updates. This is *hugely* helpful, as it forces you to be thinking about your book *constantly* without ever having any opportunity to relax or take your mind off of the project[35]. Sure, a few bad apples might want a piece of that six hundred, but it's SIX HUNDRED DOLLARS! You can split that twenty ways and everyone will still be happy. Plus, Uncle Martin acts cold and distant, but he misses you, he really does. Pick up the phone.

6.   **Cancel your doctor's appointments:** To put it simply, writing cures what ails you. You may think that sounds absurd, but there is a clear, direct link between writing and health, and no Writer has ever come down with so much as the common cold while writing. And that's just the key: WHILE writing. Taking breaks obviously opens you up to various illnesses, and going to the doctor is considered taking a break. Don't do it! That old quack's gonna pump you full of so much poison that you'll be lucky if you have a

---

[35] Relaxation is the writer's enemy.

clear idea come into your head ever again. So keep those hands moving.

7.   **Sell your home and move to a different city:** Oftentimes a change of scenery can really help a struggling writer power through and start putting words on the page. One surefire way to change up the scenery is to sell your home[36] for cheap and find a new one in a different area. The further away from friends and family the better since, even though their interest in your project is essential to your success, their proximity to you is a distraction rivaled only by the drink[37]! Pack your bags. You can obviously move back once you've written your book and made over six hundred smackers.

8.   **If you drink, become sober:** Google your favorite writers. Studies have shown that as many as 97% of all successful writers became that way by completely abstaining from alcohol. Alcohol, as we discussed in chapter

---

[36] Or break your lease.
[37] See number 7.

3, is a depressant and that means it makes you depressed and also makes you not want to write. So, who would you rather be, Jack Daniels or Jack Kerouac[38]? The choice might seem tough, but you really can't have both. Keep only the spirits that you use in your famous Zucchinana bread and dump the rest down the drain.

9. **If you're sober, start drinking[39]:** Google your favorite writers. Studies have shown that as many as 97% of all successful writers became that way by get totally annihilated every day. Alcohol, as we discussed in chapter 3, is a depressant and that means it gives you great ideas and allows you to take your mind off of that grueling shoulder pain and bang out fifteen pages, baby! Just don't drink vodka, rum, gin, cognac, bourbon, scotch, beer, wine, or spiked seltzer. The real OG writers all drank hard lemonade exclusively. And I'm not going to say exactly *whose* hard lemonade they drank, but it certainly wasn't Steve's!

---

[38] Famously sober during his entire career.
[39] Please do not break your sobriety because of my book. I'm proud of you!

10. **Play roulette:** This is clearly the most important tip we learned, I think that's safe to say. After all, what's better than a minimum of six hundred dollars? That's right, a minimum of twelve hundred dollars. In fact it's at least twice as good. And the most guaranteed, surefire way to double one's money is to put it all on RED[40]. Now, there are a few strategies that the bettors will bark at you, but I find that it's best to just keep playing your lucky number of times. Doing so thirteen[41] times in a row will earn you roughly 4.9 million dollars. If that doesn't make you want to finish writing your book, I don't know what will!

---

[40] Do not EVER "put it all on black". We didn't really go over this earlier, because I didn't think you were ready, but putting your money on black is a cursed gamble. If you don't understand why, I must implore that you familiarize yourself with the works of Robert Louis Stevenson. And, while you're at it, why don't you give old RLS a quick google image search. What a hunk, right?

[41] Every great writer's lucky number.

And there you have it, my friend. Look at your hands.

Notice anything different? No? Well you should, because they're

no longer normal hands. They are now the hands of a writer and

a damned good one. Let me just say that it's been a real pleasure

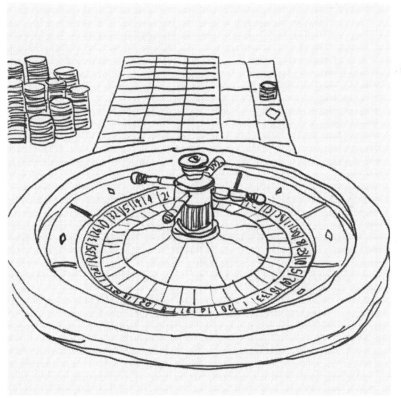

teaching you how to write a book that makes at least six

hundred dollars and I definitely don't want something horrible to

happen to you in the near future. Why would I? After all, we

90

both know that you read the whole book, in order, without

skipping around. And anyone who reads my whole book

deserves nothing but Ringo Starrian peace and love for years and

years to come. And, because you're one of those people who

read the whole book, you deserve to live a long and fruitful life

as a writer. And so you shall[42].

---

[42] My fingers are crossed as I write this entire paragraph. I am assuming the pea-brained chapter skipper won't even be reading footnotes, but this one's for the super sleuth extra credit kids who kept reading this decoy chapter just to see what happened. Good on ya.

NOTES FOR YOUR BOOK

<u>NOTES FOR YOUR BOOK</u>

NOTES FOR YOUR BOOK

NOTES FOR YOUR BOOK

NOTES FOR YOUR BOOK

NOTES FOR YOUR BOOK

NOTES FOR YOUR BOOK

NOTES FOR YOUR BOOK

NOTES FOR YOUR BOOK

NOTES FOR YOUR BOOK

NOTES FOR YOUR BOOK

NOTES FOR YOUR BOOK

NOTES FOR YOUR BOOK

NOTES FOR YOUR BOOK

NOTES FOR YOUR BOOK

NOTES FOR YOUR BOOK

NOTES FOR YOUR BOOK

NOTES FOR YOUR BOOK

NOTES FOR YOUR BOOK

NOTES FOR YOUR BOOK

NOTES FOR YOUR BOOK

NOTES FOR YOUR BOOK

NOTES FOR YOUR BOOK

NOTES FOR YOUR BOOK

NOTES FOR YOUR BOOK

NOTES FOR YOUR BOOK

NOTES FOR YOUR BOOK

NOTES FOR YOUR BOOK

NOTES FOR YOUR BOOK

NOTES FOR YOUR BOOK

NOTES FOR YOUR BOOK

NOTES FOR YOUR BOOK

NOTES FOR YOUR BOOK

NOTES FOR YOUR BOOK

NOTES FOR YOUR BOOK

NOTES FOR YOUR BOOK

NOTES FOR YOUR BOOK

NOTES FOR YOUR BOOK

NOTES FOR YOUR BOOK

NOTES FOR YOUR BOOK

NOTES FOR YOUR BOOK

NOTES FOR YOUR BOOK

NOTES FOR YOUR BOOK

NOTES FOR YOUR BOOK

NOTES FOR YOUR BOOK

Made in the USA
San Bernardino, CA
13 June 2019